FROM THE MIND OF A MAD WAM

BY

William Marshall Davis

From the Mind of a Mad WAM

© 2020 William Marshall Davis

All rights reserved. No part of this publication may be reproduced or transmitted in any form or by any means, electronic or mechanical, including photocopy, recording, or any information storage and retrieval system, without permission in writing from the publisher.

ISBN 978-1-7354026-0-4

Table of Contents

Chapter 1 — WAM's Standard Poetry

Is Your Life Nice? ~ 19

Can You Comprehend? ~ 21

With Words Spoken ~ 23

What Do You Want out of Life? ~ 25

I Never Tasted You ~ 27

Life Questions ~ 29

Romantic Psalms ~ 31

Want ~ 33

WAM Confessionals ~ 35

Fine… Is the Girl! ~ 37

I Wrote Our Names On the Wall ~ 39

How I Feel ~ 41

Why? ~ 43

Searching For My Place ~ 45

Resurrection ~ 47

The Way My Mind Functions ~ 51

Around You ~ 53

First You Must Weep ~ 55

My God ~ 59

More Than Words Can Convey ~ 61

I'll See You Through ~ 63

Respect Me ~ 65

Internal Turmoil ~ 69

The Story of a Father ~ 71

What Has This Time Done to Me? ~ 73

Pain ~ 75

This Is Inevitable ~ 77

Our Intentions ~ 79

A Woman's Power ~ 81

Vulnerability ~ 83

My Time ~ 87

Trapped ~ 91

Soul Mate ~ 93

Drug Addiction ~ 95

A Message for My Oldest Son ~ 97

Success ~ 101

Quietly Hoping ~ 103

Intimacy ~ 105

Chapter 2 — WAM's Fables

Undercover ~ 111

A Bad Dream ~ 121

Wrong Turn ~ 127

Spousal Abuse ~ 133

Me ~ 143

Afterword ~ 149

DEDICATION

This and all my future works are dedicated to the following special people. You are and always will be my motivation:

Marshall G. Arrington

Emma J. Arrington

Benjamin Crumbley

Mary Crumbley

William Micah Davis

Nasasha Roberta Davis

Abdul Malik Waleed Davis

Isaiah Ameer Davis

Also, I'd like to dedicate this book to:

Marshall Arrington Jr.

Patricia L. Boykin

Derrick Phelps

May God bless and rest the dead. I miss you all so much.

Acknowledgements

I would like to extend my special thanks and appreciation to the following special people. Without you this could not have been done. Thank you.

Literary Agent
Eartha Minniefield

Editor
Lisa R. Thomas

Cover Designer
Darnell V. Wilson

Typist
Shanda Edmondson

Publishing Editor
Daniel Halpern

Acknowledgments

The following people were there from the start of this journey and played a very important part. Thank you.

Ryan Hourigan

Katrina Rodgers

Leah Campbell

CHRISTINA YELENIC

A VERY SPECIAL THANK YOU FOR AFFORDING ME THE OPPORTUNITY TO OBTAIN AN UNDERSTANDING OF LIFE ONLY WORTHY OF GOD'S AND MEN OF GOD.

THANK YOU SO VERY MUCH.

AUTHOR'S NOTE

Well here it is—my first book! It took six years to be exact and it is finally done. For me, it took too long, but that was due to my being a novice to the writing game.

My plan is to continue writing and produce more books, as writing brings me joy. From this book, I have obtained a feeling of great accomplishment and self-worth. I am so proud to have started and completed this project that, even if I never sell a copy or receive monetary reward, it won't matter. If it be the will of God, my prayer is that I regain the respect and admiration of my family. May they come to understand my journey, my past in particular, and grow to appreciate the man I am today.

For you, the reader, it is my hope that through my writing you will feel, understand, and relate to my struggle, pain, and growth. Hard as it is for me, I am breaking myself open. Making myself vulnerable by revealing my innermost self in hopes that my writing will be felt, for they are real. This is why I chose the expression of poetry, for it is the speaker to the rhythm of the heart, no matter the rate of the beat. May the food I provide, through my words nourish your minds, hearts and souls.

Thank You.

WAM'S STANDARD POETRY

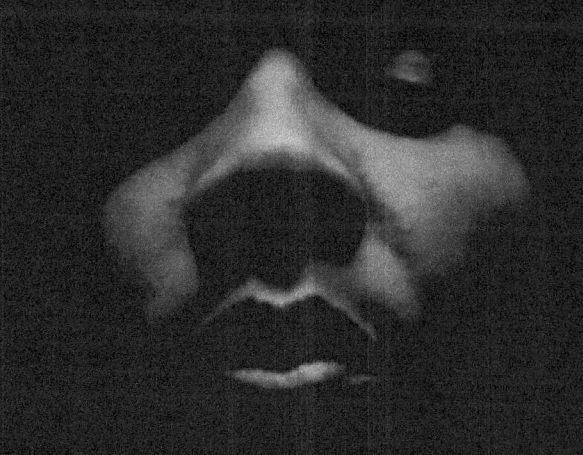

Is Your Life Nice?

You probably feel as if your life is nice

But what I offer you is paradise and the title of my wife

That comes with the promise of I'll always be there

Not out with the boys or involved in extramarital affairs

Exotic trips to exotic lands

For you, I'll be God's prototype of what's called a "real man"

I'll go above and beyond to show you I care

Like paying attention to detail and love making, *le extraordinaire!*

I will release you of all your fears

And never, to your rebuttal, I will turn a deaf ear

Other women will not get my first look

And I will be receptive to your input

Together, we will laugh until we cry

The two of us apart, would be a sheer disaster

But I am sure that we'll be together in the hereafter

Because not even the roughest weather

Could blow apart what God has put together

And I want you to know, that for you, I'll make any sacrifice

Even though, right now you probably feel as if your life is nice.

Can You Comprehend?

These words that I write,

Are you mature enough to comprehend?

Are you woman enough to be my true friend?

For me, will you remove your seven veils?

And will you be there for me when all else fails?

Does your love and devotion have a cost?

If so, how much shall I pay you for you to help me when I feel lost?

When I feel afraid and want to run and hide

Will you stand by me holding my hand, being my guide?

If I cry in front of you, will you laugh?

Tell me, are you capable of being my better half?

When I am pursued and tormented by my enemies,

Will you be brave enough to protect me?

Can I be the man you undisputedly choose?

What I'm asking, is will you fight with me win or lose?

Will you attempt to fix me when I'm broke?

And when I feel desolate, will you help me find hope?

If I should yield to the winds of powerful storms,

Will you comfort me and make me feel warm?

Can you make me believe that one day my troubles will end?

These words that I write,

Are you mature enough to comprehend?

With Words Spoken

With a minimal amount of words spoken

You've got this thug's nose wide open

But, I have limited amounts of time to myself to give

So I can't allow myself to succumb to the octaves

It's true, that you have a silky seductiveness to your voice

But this thug is choosy about his final choice

Keep in mind I'm talking about my choice of friends

Do know my means will justify my ends

Your views and points I am intrigued by them

But girlfriend, I will not fall victim

So come correct or please don't come

Because I am not deaf and blind nor am I dumb

The imperfection of human beings can make life hard

And oh, my wrath is only matched by that of God's

Our pasts, I chose to call "way back when"

Now the slate is clear, so let this affinity begin

And please, remember that my intention's not husband and wife

But maybe just maybe, we can help each other do this thing called "life"

Understand that I will not become one of your tokens

Just because of the minimal among your words that were spoken.

What Do You Want out of Life?

Tell me lady, what do you want out of life?

Do you want to be a career girl or maybe a housewife?

Or perhaps you'll choose to live your life in segregated segments,

But, I think you'll look beautiful barefoot and pregnant

Tell me, what do you expect from your man?

Do you need him to be your groupie or just an ordinary everyday fan?

I can't imagine you invading the corporate world

With your pigtails and baby doll curls

Lady, when is the last time you achieved one of your goals?

Throughout life, love will be lost

But, if you allow me to, I'll help you bear your cross

I'd be less of a man to attempt to choose for you a direction

I'm man enough to provide for you loyalty and protection

What I'm saying is, that in this world of so much hate,

I'll be your cloak, dagger, and your means of shelter and escape

I'll also help you fight all of life's adversities

Because lady, that's how much you mean to me

You absolutely have to be woman enough to deal with life's stress and strife

So, tell me lady, what do you want out of life?

I Never Tasted You

It's true, you I've never tasted,

Though on you, my precious words have been wasted

Not to mention my mind's time

For some reason, I was temporarily blind

I curse the day I first heard your name

And I curse the womb from which you came

But I alone, hold the blame

Effortlessly, I gave my willingness to be used in vain

You made me sightless with your shine,

Though once or twice, I've seen your kind

Your kind is what I call the "tall grass"

I classify you below the lower class

The way you act is why I negatively react

I believe you weren't born,

Your snake-ass was hatched

But, the God in me makes me check my manners

And the man in me makes me check my grammar

So, I won't belittle you with insults

But, you brought about the end results

In truth, there's no time wasted

But, I'm sad because you I've never tasted.

Life Questions

I don't have answers or solutions

And before January's half over,

I've already broken my New Year's Resolutions

I don't care about global warming or acid rain,

I'm in need of something to get rid of this emotional pain

My life hurts so badly at times

I look in the mirror at my goatee and notice gray hair

Wondering when or how the fuck they got there

I know I got to find my soul

Because all of a sudden I got old

They say with gray comes wisdom

Is that why in the past I acted so dumb,

Because I didn't have none?

So, here I am still around in the year 2002

Thirty-six years old and I still don't know what to do

Stuck in a void of problems, and confusion

My mom says pray to God

I'm starting to wonder if there is one

This God of ours must charge a fee—

Or maybe it's just that he don't like me

I've read the Quran and the Bible more than twice

So why am I treated like the Anti-Christ?

All I want out of life is to be on good terms with my father and mother

And secure a future for my oldest son,

His younger sister and little brothers

Mom suggests rehabilitation

That's not one of my expectations

So as puppies turn to dogs and cats from kittens

You can't change your life, because it's already been written.

Romantic Psalms

I just want to hold you and kiss your eyelids

Maybe go to a park and run around as if we were young kids

I haven't done little simple stuff, like that with a woman in a while

I just want to see you laugh and on your face a smile

To hear pleasure in your voice when I call

The way you say yes when I offer to take you to the mall

With how complicated life gets

We need to know there's so much more to life than casual sex

I have to truly know a woman in order to love her

What's the use of intercourse if I have to wear a rubber?

There's much importance in a kiss or a touch

Soft, romantic words that cause her to blush

Nicknames like "sweetheart" and "boo"

You can never say too many I love you's

Be a gentleman and help her take off her coat

Every now and then, leave her a love note

You can be traditional with candy, cards, and flowers

Or you can dress her in silk,

Buy her expensive perfume and exotic body powders

What makes women overwhelmed with pleasure and joy

Is to be looked upon as more than a man's toy

There's extraordinary power in a thing called romance

If you base your relationship on it, you'll give it a fighting chance

Me myself, I cater to the needs of my woman

I make her feel as if I'm her number one fan

Make every day feel like the first day you met

You won't believe how strong your relationship will get

When a man meets a woman his first thought should be a ring

Cause a good woman is truly a special thing.

Want

In a crowd of over a million women

I could still pick out your face

Take me by the hand and lead me to your most private place

I love to feel the softness of your outer covering

The depth of your eyes, keeps me constantly wondering

I'm not a man concerned with the sign of your zodiac

True we are different,

It is said opposites attract

When you're around me time seems to stop

I daydream about making love to you on a snow-capped mountain top

Or better yet, under a waterfall named Niagara

I want to satisfy you so bad; I'm taking Viagra

I want you to be my pill called "ecstasy"

Your femininity and sexuality bring out the best in me

I know that you'll be overly pleasing to my taste buds

But, what I'm hoping is that we could fall deeply in love

In the physical, but the mental aspect of

In-depth conversations and intense back rubs

I want to be the reason you want to live

God knows I want to be the father of your kids

In no way am I close to perfect

In this ignorant world of one night stands

Would you mind being my woman?

Because I damn sure want to be your man

I wish to share more than what's accepted as normal

Something between us, we can consider very special

Yeah in a crowd of over a million women I can still smell your fragrance

When I'm alone, I can even sense your presence

Still, I want you to lead me by the hand to your most private place

And you need to do it soon 'fore we have no more time to waste.

WAM Confessionals

I've lived a life full of lies

How I squint because truth hurts my eyes

I was always trying to be who the next person wanted me to be

When all I had to do was be me

Always trying to keep up with a phantom named Jones

I always wound up with scars and broken bones

Fell victim for every gimmick and fad

Never content with the good shit I had

Through all my struggles and all my toils

To my own self I couldn't even be loyal

A partaker in the art of self-murder

Somewhat of a sellout and family deserter

The good Lord knows I've tried

And my cheeks still burn from the tears I cried

Don't misunderstand this is not a sympathy plea

Just a troubled man's shot at sincerity

I hear the call from graves that have been dug

And I wonder why I was so unreceptive to all the love

I was truly the exception to all the rules

But, because of no discipline, I became the accepted fool

Who would believe me, falling victim to pharmaceuticals?

The one who did above average in high school

My Life leaves many shaking their heads

Not because of what I've done

But because I'm not already dead

I've had people tricked into thinking I'm intelligent,

With a Master's Degree in Criminal Confinement

I hope through my problems a message is sent,

Sometimes, I talk good shit when I decide to vent.

Fine... Is the Girl!

Have you ever seen a girl,

That makes you bite the palm of your hand?

I mean one that makes you say

Words like *shit* and *got damn?*

You're sure God's sending you a direct sign

I know one that coos when she talks

Her pussy tickles her thighs when she walks

Because every time I see her she's smiling

And every time I'm scheming a midnight fling

All bright eyed with dimples so simply cute,

Breath smells like berries and exotic fruits

The kind of woman you would take home to mother

But first you go home and kill all your brothers

I know the girl that you just want to touch and hold

A little knock-kneed and a bit pigeon-toed

When she sweats it smells like chiffon,

Long silky hair and shaved underarms

Yeah, this girl is *madd tuff*

And everything she wears turns into hot stuff

But I am telling you if you ever run across a girl

That makes you bite the palm of your hand,

Do all you can to be her man.

I Wrote Our Names on the Wall

Today, I wrote our names on the wall

Nothing spectacular, just a little black ink that's all

But it was my personal way of rededicating me to you

And in my position, I couldn't think of anything else to do

But there is, for all to see

Telling the World that I belong to you and you belong to me

Actually, I think that it looks kind of nice

Nice enough to make the average person look twice

The women who may see it say, "Oh that's so romantic and sweet!"

Look, their names complement each other, because they are so unique

We need to give this relationship a fighting chance

Because our names are so full of meaning and substance,

Not to mention, the way you feel about me and the way I feel about you

Close your eyes, my love,

Envision all the beautiful things in life we could do

From day one, your name has been written in my heart

And I hope that mine is in yours,

If not in total,

Then

At least in part

If it's not, I won't act like I don't care

I'll just continue to have faith and put in work,

Until it's permanently there

Right now, I want to grab the telephone and make a call

Oh, did I tell you that today

I wrote our names on the wall.

How I Feel

Obviously, you don't understand how I feel

So now it's time I tell you the deal

There's something that you don't realize about me

And that is, I could care less about your pussy

Tho' true, I'm lured by your sex appeal

I'm more concerned about you being real

Believe me, when I say that life is not a game

And the emotion called love is born in the center of your brain

I refuse to be seduced by your female toxins

What I want you to do is open your heart and let me in

Why won't you allow me to explore your mind?

Are you ashamed of what I might find?

As far as you're concerned, you're a star by far

Or are you embarrassed by who you really are?

Can't you see what the world is doing to you?

It has reduced you to accepting face value

I can't promise you

How much longer I'll be around

And I'm not sure what you've lost

But I am indeed what you have found

Soon, on my heart there will be an unbreakable seal

Because obviously, you don't understand how I feel.

Why

Why are you so afraid of me?

Because God blessed me with a little size and muscular strength?

But, know that he also made me wise and gave me the ability to think

Why do you avoid me?

Is it because of my ever-growing intellect?

Or the fact that my character commands respect?

Why do you down me?

Maybe it's because I'm not with the negative things you choose,

Or the fact that I refuse to ever take a chance to lose

Why are you so scared of me?

Because I'm not gonna be anybody's token

My views and opinions are gonna be loudly spoken

Why do you want to lock me up?

Because I want to do something to change my luck

And I no longer want to live a life that's corrupt?

Why do you want to kill me?

Because I no longer want to settle

But strive for a much higher level?

Why do you want to destroy me?

Could it be because I want more for my family?

And I want to be the best man I can possibly be?

All I'm wanting to do is give something positive a try

So, can you please, just explain to me—why?

Searching For My Place

Inside I hurt so much

So, I pray to the Lord for my soul to be touched

There's so much confusion in this man's brain

And I'm in so much mental pain

My life has been surrounded by anguish

Please, tell me what is the meaning of all of this?

If my dear momma made me good

Then, why am I so misunderstood?

I try to walk the fine line

But all I seem to do is waste my life and time

I know that this life I harbor is only a rental

But is the God that I worship judgmental?

I live like a *Gorilla in the Mist*

And at times, I want to slit my wrists

Tho' armor-coated is my insides

I'm too wise to commit suicide

But I'll be alright if God is truly just

I'm still wondering who I should trust

What I have is the opposite of the Midas touch

I guess that's why I hurt so much.

Resurrection

The world is a cave and my mind is my home

And only me alone, can move the heavy stone

This whole process has taken longer than three days,

It's gonna take long to resurrect the dead slave

Jesus, the Christ, came back in the flesh,

But mental resurrection is the only way we'll make any progress

I strive for education and to be my own boss

To right myself from an upside-down cross

Wanting to be perfect, my dialogue and my diction

To avoid stoning and a modern-day crucifixion

I'm learning from the ones who were great, but I want to do more

No disrespect intended to Martin, Malcolm and Tupac Shakur

My mind set is to give rebirth to intellects

To teach self-discipline, self-worth, and self-respect

See I'm tired of living on my knees

Tired of holding onto religious prophecies

I can't continue to uplift ordinary men

Because that keeps me torn between concepts of spiritual doctrines

Like I said, it's gonna take longer to resurrect the dead slave

And my hands are gonna have to get dirty,

Digging my way out of the grave

Society, in itself is a closed casket—

So I fight for life, rather than submit

In the quiet of the night, I hear my own eulogy

I'm physically alive, but the ash and dust cover me

The world is a cave and the stone has been my protection,

I'm no longer afraid, so now is the time for my resurrection.

The Way My Mind Functions

It's very complex the way my mind functions

Because sometimes I draw the wrong conclusions or make the wrong assumptions

Every now and then I go a little crazy…

But rest assured, when in my proper mind

A better man than me, you will rarely find

My want is for you to forgive me

And know, from my heart, I extend my most humble apology

Because ever since that day, I've had nothing but regrets

And ever since that day, I haven't stopped kicking myself in the ass yet

I'm asking you to, please, not hate me for being overly brash

And find it within your heart to let the past be the past

My personality is hard and my character intense—

But I promise that, if given the chance,

One day all of this will make sense

You'd best believe that there's plenty of method to my madness

Now, at this point a crucial decision lies in your hands

I would not be writing this poem if I did not give a damn

So I swear that my intentions were not to push any negative buttons…

Sometimes I can't control the way my mind functions.

Around You

It's around you that this man's world revolves

And it's with you that this man wants to evolve

Build our relationship into a dynasty

Just you, me, and maybe some babies

This is what I love about you most

Your character and attitude inspire mental development and spiritual growth

You create in me this joyful sensation

In you, I envision this rock-solid foundation

Your body scent breathes of dedication and devotion

Your breath's fragrance fills the air with feeling and emotion

You constantly keep me in the mind of kisses and holding hands

I'm proud that you chose me to be your man

The power that your womanly essence emits

Makes me realize that with you there are no limits

So together we can reach the sky

And in each other find the answer to the question
"Why?"

You are the definition of sincere intent

You are the target of my loving sentiments

Because of you, my past problems have been solved

It is around you that this man's world revolves.

First You Must Weep

Before you dry another's eyes, first you must weep

Because your brother's soul is your own soul to keep

Let me not live a life that's free

Unless I'm doing things to bring my spirit closer to "Thee"

How can I hope to ever physically heal?

The mental wounds of others that I do not feel

How am I to know what my brother truly needs?

If I've never tilled his garden or sown his seeds?

Who am I to close my eyes and pretend not to see

And what kind of man would I be if I turned a deaf ear to a beggar's plea?

If I think that I'm weak whenever I am kind

Then I am no better than a spirit who is deaf, dumb, and blind,

We live day to day in the realm of spiritual science

And choose not to follow His almighty supreme guidance

So who will help you carry the burden of your cross?

When you have yet to realize, you alone are not your own boss

No one is worthy to be spared heartache and sorrow

For those who build the willpower to get up and try again tomorrow

So you pray for one's soul before you go to sleep

But before you dry another's eyes first, you must weep.

My God

Something is wrong with this prodigy

But still, my God chooses to shine on me

Because when I've fallen and I'm lost

God picks me up, shows me the way and brushes me off

At times it's hard to save face

But I do because of God's amazing grace

And every time I think this life is over

I feel God's loving, caring hand upon my shoulder

Then, I hear God's voice in my ear

Saying, "Be strong, hold your faith son, and have no fear"

So I press on just one more day

And I continue to fall on my knees and pray

When I pray, I give thanks

To let God know I want to be a soldier within the ranks

Because I'm tired of doing wrong for so long

I want to be right with God when this life is gone

So the righteous direction I search to find

And keep God conscious at all times in my mind

Even though I feel something's wrong with this prodigy

Still, God chooses to shine on me.

More Than Words Can Convey

I love you more than words could ever convey

So cut my heart out of my chest and keep it

It belongs to you anyway

You are the sole object of all my devotion

Your movement, whether standing or sitting is poetry in motion

I think that you are as cute as a black Barbie

I'm wondering, will you ever belong to me?

Because I'm building me a doll collection

And you'll be my one and only prize possession

I promise to take care of you from your head to your feet

And keep you until you become an old antique

But seriously, you're the doll that I want to keep in my house

And yours is the tongue I want in my mouth

I never truly understood this love hype

Until you became part of my life

I've been trying to make sense of the way I feel

And my senses tell me that what I feel is real

I don't want to share this love with no other

I want you to be my wife and my children's mother

I don't know what else I could say

Except I love you, more than words could ever convey.

I'll See You Through

Grab my love and I'll see you through

Because I know that sometimes you need something to hold onto

There's no guarantee that overnight the bad times will stop

But, until they do, I'll be your well-grounded rock

I don't have all the answers to all your questions why

But I have a strong shoulder for you to use should you want to cry.

I have no idea as to when your struggle will end

But I want you to find comfort in the fact that I'll always be your friend

If you need me, just open your heart and talk…

And when you are lonely, hold my hand in your mind and take a walk

What I'm saying is that when you feel so alone

Let the thought of my dedication place you in a comfort zone

When you pray to God for days that are sunny and new

Feel me because I'm right there on my knees praying with you

I'll help you to stand fast when you want to flee

And if you don't believe in anything else, please believe in me

So remember my written words letter to the letter…

If you allow them to, things can't help but get better

To be strong is what I so dearly want you to do

Until you can grab my love and I'll see you through.

Respect Me

It's not a must that you like what you see

But it is mandatory that, at all cost, you respect me

All that making derogatory remarks under your breath

And more or less playing WAM to the left,

Will most definitely be laid to rest

See, I only want in everything I do to be the very best

Or…should I settle for failure, is that what you suggest?

Once again I'm WAM,

I am what I am

And that's all I am

I really don't give a damn

If you are foe or fan

With all that's left in me

I'm gonna remain a man

For I've seen far too much violence

And not nearly enough peace

So if you continue to disrespect me I will unleash the beast

What I'm saying is WAM wants to live his life right

But one thing WAM can and will do is fight

Respect commands respect, so that's exactly what you'll get

If you don't give it back, expect to get severely checked

Treat WAM like you want to be treated

If you can't do that, your whole purpose is defeated

I am blessed by God that's true enough

Gifted with the quickness to call one's bluff

I'd rather die standing than to live on my knees

I hope I don't have to show you to make you believe

WAM's gonna get his proper due

From no matter who—it's my will or you are through

This is not conceit, it's confidence

From a man who relies on common sense

I just want to contribute something legendary to people of the world

As one of God's imperfect creations, I realize I could fall easily

But while I'm standing, make sure that you respect me.

Internal Turmoil

I try to hold onto my mental stability

But still, insanity slowly keeps taking control of me

I feel a form of Schizophrenia that's chronic

Or could it be that I'm possessed by something demonic?

Whatever the case, something is definitely wrong

Something bad is bound to happen, before long

Mom asks dad, "What's wrong with him?"

He says, "There's probably a crack in his brain stem!"

They say, "He was a good boy, but now breaks the rules"

"He doesn't act like himself," maybe possessed by something evil

This voice in my head, how can I stop it?

Maybe I need the drugs they call psychotropic?

'Cause my attitude is one that's psychotic

God, what am I, a hopeless neurotic?

Running in and out of realms of reality

I'm a walking, breathing, human catastrophe

I'm slowly but surely coming unglued

I need something to alter my mind and my mood

This is draining me of all my energy, this trying to hold onto my mental stability.

The Story of a Father

Do you know the story of your father?

Let me tell you who he is

He blends words together with a delicate harmony

What this means is your father writes beautiful poetry

Daily, working out to maintain his health

Because he doesn't want you being raised by anyone else

Then, he wasn't there for you as a child

Now he plans on staying around for a while

He no longer enjoys the pleasure of the bottle

And some younger people even call him a role model

True, he was a bad seed way back then

Now he's a leader among men

No longer partaking in temptations, he shuns them.

And they call him Waleed Abdul Muhaymin because he is a Muslim

He stands six foot four and a half inches tall

All he wants to do is be there for you

And he will if it's the last thing he'll ever do

So the next time someone tries to tell you who your father was

You can tell them what your father now does.

What Has This Time Done to Me?

God, what has this time done to me?

I feel like I'm going absolutely crazy

See, I feel like at any moment I'll blow

Why? I can't say for I don't know

I'm just tired of all that has been done to me

Moving just beyond the point of being enraged

From being treated like a boy who's been bad

What I am is a grown man who's fighting mad

How much more can a man take and at what point will he break?

Tell me, what right does two wrongs make?

Inside me is what it takes to become great

Yet I'm being forced to cultivate my hate

I'm feeling pushed to fight

And I want to do just that because things aren't right

I feel as if I have no options left

And have become fearfully unafraid of death

Tho' the complete opposite is what I prefer

I've been transferred into a vicious, violent ferocious monster

When I close my eyes I see a repeat of history

So tell me God, what has this time done to me?

Pain

Oh, you might know a little about physical pain

If you fell down a flight of stairs, broke your neck, and forgot your name

You still wouldn't experience half the pain that swells my chest and fills my brain

I'd rather break my neck than to have this mental pain I go through

Like having your firstborn never speak or say, "I love you"

Pain, because the youngest son you never see

Is more than likely calling another man his daddy

Or how about this?

You make another baby by another lady

And without knowing that lady has moved to another city with your unborn baby

Pain is living in fear

Of the monkey on the attack

Always returning to live on my back

Pain is the daughter, who loves you with all her heart

Although she tries to be strong because the things you do tear her apart

Mom and step-dad love me, but all I do is make them frown

Every time I come around them I always seem to pull them down

You ever wonder as a small infant what could you do

To make your biological father want to have nothing to do with you?

Pain is grandma and grandad who worship each hair on my head

And you probably won't get your life together until they are both dead

Skeletons in their closets most people have

Well, that ain't shit 'cause my room looks like *Valley of Dry Bones*

Do you know the pain of being able to be whatever you wanted to be

But you have reduced yourself to a person who commits felony after felony?

Is there a pill to ease this pain?

I'm so tired of living in pain

I guess it's time for me to do what I can to change.

This is Inevitable

You know how some things are just meant to be?

Well, two of these things are you and me

You can fight hard, but the fight won't be long

Because I'm the one you think about when you hear a love song

See, I'm like a deadly virus

And once we come together there is no separating us

I am now a major part of your blood

And the next step is you're gonna fall in love

You can shake your head and say that you are not

But once your feelings are moving in that direction, they're going to be hard to stop

I'm the one that makes you realize that you can

And I'm everything that you have ever wanted in a man

The others fill your heart with doubt

But I'm the one you always dream about

You can carry on like you don't know

That this is like a fungus, it can't help but grow

So you can run but you can't hide

And you sure can't fight the way you feel inside

When you close your eyes, I know it's my face that you see

And you know that some things were just meant to be.

Our Intentions

Exactly what are we attempting to create?

Something real or something fake?

The basis I'm on is a need-to-know

Will what we share be stunted or will we give it what it needs to grow?

Sincere or bull?

Something ugly or something beautiful?

Am I left to wonder and guess?

Is my answer no or is it yes?

What God has placed before us is just a test

Will we be at our worse or at our best?

I'm also wondering, can we do the time?

And can we stay fresh in each other's mind?

Could we be touched by each other's spirit?

You're not here but when you speak, I hear it

Could what I feel be considered true love?

Because you're the only woman that I think of

Only the creator knows our intents

But I alone know the object of our sentiments

To see the total picture, I guess I'll have to wait

But you still need to tell me what we are attempting to create.

A Woman's Power

You are a woman and you are beautiful too

And I long to explore the spiritual aspects of you

In you, there is so much energy

I wish that I was a scientist

So I could experiment with your chemistry

Parts of you are unexplored like outer space

And there are so many parts of you that we men waste

You are the reason flowers bloom

And nuclear power lives in your womb

Because of you so much progress has been made

It's a blessing to be invited to your brain waves

Of activities that take place at night

Life comes from you and then grows to full light

The knowledge, at your feet lies in abundance

Not to mention the luxury of your kiss and a slow dance

If a man truly took time to get to know you

So quickly would he speak the words I do

For a man to mistreat you is to deny himself

All of the world's riches and his inner wealth

To research you, men would find this to be true

You are a woman and beautiful too.

Vulnerability

I want for me and you to be

But I'm not trying to fall victim to my vulnerability

See, my pride makes me feel like less than a man

Especially when I tell you that you have my heart in your hands

Should I grow my hair and put on a skirt?

I'm afraid of failure and being hurt

To me, this is one of life's many mysteries

How can a man be beaten by his sensitivities?

What I'm saying is that life in itself is rough

So will the love that we share between us be enough?

There is so much involved in good relations

Like devotion, dedication and top shelf communication

But do we possess those necessary traits?

And to see shall we be patient enough to wait?

Understand that I long to taste your lips and tongue

At the same time I want to turn tail and run.

But I will stand and with my fear I'll fight

Because the truth be told, I love you with all my might

Please don't feel as if I'm engulfed with negativity

Because I do want for you and me to be.

My Time

I occupy my time in many different ways

Being confined you have some good and bad days

I'm here strictly of my own accord

But I'm alive because of the grace of my Lord

So I am in no way sad

I am alive and breathing

So for that I'm glad

I often reflect on the pleasurable times that I've had

And find some good in every bad

So good is what I look for

And when I find some, I look for more

Because all is not lost until they nail the coffin lid shut

And I'm here writing, so that could be called good luck

This blessed time I take and maximize

And I try to make some truth out of all the lies

Sometimes, I dwell on the time I waste

And try hard to hold onto my faith

Because at this point faith is all that I have

And I'll admit that sometimes it gets hard to smile and laugh

But when I don't want to do just that

And at no time do I cut me any slack

So while I'm in here I have some good and bad days

And I'll occupy my time in many different ways.

Trapped

I've been trapped in my own hell
Now, they got me locked up in a cell
At times, I wonder where the time was spent
For my crimes, this is part of my punishment
Inside I cry, so I don't share my tears
And I act tough, so I don't show my fears
The illusion of my being outspoken
Hides that I am one break from being broken
For redemption, what's it going to take?
Really, what kind of sense does this make?
You yourself are creating your own illusions
Profiting from the less fortunate ones
Tell me who can I call upon?
When my religious beliefs are all but gone
And I'm wondering will I be here long
See I can't sleep because the lights are always on
Through the glass I question all of you
But I'll do this time until my time is through
Lift my head to the heavens and say, "Oh well"
Because I'm still trapped in my own hell.

Soul Mate

Even though we are miles apart—

If l listen to the wind

I can hear the rhythm of your heart

I get power from the strength of its beat

Then I became frightened and within myself, I retreat

I find courage knowing that you'll always belong to me

No matter where on God's earth you might be

Right now, you might be in the arms of another man

But that surface shit don't mean a damn!

Because I know it's me that's in your bones

And I'm the drug your body jones

Anything else is not treats but tricks

For it's me who gives you the real fix

Look at yourself and tell the truth

Every other man in your life has been a sugar substitute

Knowing someday I'll come back has you consistently paranoid

But quiet as it's kept, no one else can fill your void

Yes, I admit, I put you through pure hell

With my issues, so obviously hidden that you could not tell

Now you hear me in every love song

See me in every television show

I know the longer I stay away

That you will come and find me, one day

Because you can't keep away what's real

And you can't hide the way you feel

To my problems, you had not been sympathetic

Play hard as steel but baby, I'm magnetic

You can't hide from yourself all of your life—

One day, I'll be your husband and you'll be my wife.

Drug Addiction

If you think AIDS is a serious physical condition

Try being cursed with the affliction of drug addiction

It's a disease that kills you more while you live

And it takes more than you'll ever have to give

It's a phantom that destroys families

And is the topic of so many personal tragedies

It has taken from the rich and made them poor

And when you don't have it to give

You'll find a way to give it more

It causes precious flowers not to grow

And turns beautiful women into substance ho's

It's taken precious mothers' only sons

And turned them into convicted felons

It's been known to drive a sane man crazy

And causes the womb to abort its babies

I've never seen a thing more wicked

It bounces at you like a fiendish ball, but you won't be able to kick it

It will cause you all the problems you can endure

And from what I hear, there is no cure

If you smoke, shoot, or put something in your nose

It will turn you into the me nobody knows

It robs you of your human soul

Drug addiction is the sister to HIV

They are one in the same

You've got to believe me

Ways have been tried to stop addiction's sad transfiguration

Like detox centers and places of rehabilitation.

Yeah, I can't think of a more crippling condition

Than the one mentioned above—drug addiction.

A Message for My Oldest Son

What's up, son?

This is your daddy

I'd like to begin by first saying that I'm sorry

I feel so bad for all the wrong I've done

You deserve so much more,

Because you were my first one

I was so proud when you first came

That I blessed you with my entire name

What makes it ironic

We even look the same

Daddy has been suffering from a stroke of bad luck

But, truth be told, I just can't seem to grow up

I may not show it but I love you with all my heart

And I suffer a thousand deaths every day we are apart

I remember changing your diapers as a baby

Now I can't face you, I know you hate me

You're seventeen years old, short of being a young man

And it seems there's nothing I can do to make you understand

The pain that I feel hurts deep to the bone

But one day soon, you'll have a son of your own

Micah, I love and miss you

Though your daddy has had to deal with some major issues

I don't want you to ever feel this is your fault

And one day soon, we are going to have a man-to-man talk

But until that day you continue to live

And maybe find it in your heart one day to forgive

I'm working on a way to distance myself from the negative crowd

And working even harder to make you proud

You're probably saying you're tired of me lying

But I'll be a father to you one day or—die trying

Well son, I guess I'll bring this message to an end

If you won't let me be your father

Maybe you'll let me be your friend.

Success

What makes a man stand tall and push out his chest?

Knowing deep inside that his life has become a success

People get pleasure from counting those dollars and cents

But real pleasure comes from counting your personal accomplishments

The road to success is sometimes quite rocky—

But real men say, "I'm determined and won't let nothing stop me!"

The quest for success might be rough when you first begin—

If you fall off that horse, you have to get up and ride him again

Inside every man and woman there's this burning need

And at all cost, the Human Being wants to succeed

From the time a man is a small infant

It's already part of his nature to be triumphant.

You have to strive every day and give your best

That's the formula for *S. U. C. C. E. S. S.*—

The twist and turns life takes might drive a person nuts

But if you want to be successful, you must be strong and never give up

Do you know what goes hand in hand with being successful?

The people of the world will treat you respectful

Nothing smells better than the sweet smell of success

You can live where you want,

Have what you want

And wear the best when you dress

When they finally lay your soul to rest

You'll rest much better knowing that you lived as a success

If there's one thing in life I would suggest

Is to do all you can to grab hold of success

If you see me running around yelling *Yes, Yes, Yes*

I haven't gone crazy, what I've done is become a success.

Quietly Hoping

I loved your style and peeped your game

Please tell me, where you're from and what's your name?

See, I've been watching you for a very long time

And I can't seem to get you out of my mind

Every time you are close there is this fragrance in the air

I can't help myself when I stop and stare

I'm building my courage up to ask you for your number

But I don't want to freeze up and cause you to wonder

What can I do to grab your attention?

And if I struck up a conversation would you even listen?

Girl, you got me open twenty-four seven, like a mini mart

I want to tell you, but I don't know where to start

I figure myself as being a cool guy

But every time I approach you, I get all warm and shy

When I attempt to speak, I get all tongue-tied

Sometimes I get so nervous I just want to run and hide

I try to figure from what planet you were sent

Young, pretty, fine, and I know you are intelligent

I'm gonna see a doctor and get me some brave pills

Because I need something that's gonna give me the will

The way you walk, the way you dress

I got to believe this pressure that's building in my chest

When you're talking to your girlfriends, I hear your lovely voice

Big, beautiful eyes and damn, your lips are moist

You got me all worked up, but still I try to remain calm

You give me cottonmouth and sweaty palms

Yeah, my mind's made up and it's you that I'm choosing

It's just that when I step to you, I hope you're not refusing.

Intimacy

Most people don't take intimacy seriously

That is, most people except for me

See, I constantly search for sensual things to say

And different methods of performing foreplay

I especially like touching and kissing

Before actual penetration, she's already climbing the ceiling

I'm a man who believes the hype

And know that real women go for the romantic type

I like cunnilingus and fellatio

Nothing wrong with a little head, don't you know.

I'm about business, I do have class

But if she's right and tight, I've been known to eat a little ass

That's why the woman bum rush me

Because I'm straight out nasty

But seriously I do like intimacy

I do whatever it takes to make her fall in love with me

I make a relationship seem appealing

Being oh so attentive to her womanly feelings

Playing games like truth or dare

Washing and combing and conditioning her pubic hair

Intimacy at its best

Sucking her nipples and massaging her chest

Through good and bad—struggles and toils

Sex toys and hot body oils

This I speak is *dead for real*

I honestly care about how my woman feels

So remember this in times of great privacy

Be patient in love and exercise some intimacy.

Wam's Fables

Undercover

First let me say this story ends in tragedy

About a young, black man, new graduate from the FBI Academy

There was absolutely no way for him to know

He was what the world calls *gung ho*

Overachiever, top of his class

He thought he was doing the speed limit, but he was going way too fast

He was quite confused, to say the very least

Under the employ of the beast, a damn black police

Not once did he realize his life was on consignment

No love for himself he chose undercover work as his permanent assignment

Undercover work entails many different fields

He could have went undercover investigating crooked business deals

He could have investigated crooked politicians, giving babies kisses and hugs

But he chose to go undercover, in the dangerous world of drugs

Now why on earth would he ever go and do that?

Because straight out of the gate he cut himself no slack

Launching himself straight into hell

But he wasn't afraid of the devil, he was trained very well

He was prepared to do things that were unethical

Backed by a system that was highly technical

Little did he know he was only a puppet on a string

Following orders, waiting for the fat lady to sing

He swore an oath to himself to be the very best

And put the "ever-growing" drug trade firmly to rest

That statement, in itself was a hysterical joke

Because the world functions on the sale and resale of coke

He was brainwashed into thinking that he could actually make a change

But to the FBI he was only a badge number

No face no name

Equipped with devices of all kinds and sorts

They dropped like a bomb into a city called New York

He was supplied with weapons of all varieties at his immediate disposal

To destroy the New York drug cartel, was his proposal

Little did he know he was already dead

Thought he was Superman because he was a Fed

Though he didn't wear spandex nor a red cape

What he did have was a destiny, with a fucked-up fate

With his wired cameras and phone taps

His lightning fast reflexes and super-fast brain synapses

But all that wouldn't prove to be nearly enough

And the road he was headed down would truly be rough

His plan was to make himself a mirage

A camouflage, part of the drug cartel's entourage

His plan was not to have any actual hands-on

But to be tight with the boss, like he was his firstborn

Yeah, he figured if he was to sink a battleship

He and the big man would have to have an intimate relationship

He had to be trusted with the cartel's bylaws and policies

Because this thing wasn't just local, it was also overseas

He knew that in order to take down the big man

He had to become like the fingers

On big man's right hand

Now, I'm not exactly sure how the police got down

But he started hanging out with the largest cartel in town

In no time he became a well-known face

He and the cartel were seen all over the place

Quickly he caught the vapors

He and the big boys' pictures on the front of the local newspapers

He had all the local authorities mixed up and confused

Constantly wondering in what capacity was he being used?

Of this operation, the local police were not a part

For this operation, you see

They had to be kept in the total dark

Together, he and the cartel took trips around the world

And together they freaked exotic foreign girls

They were quite a sight for the eyes to see

Wearing designer clothes bought in the hills of Beverly

They wore shoes made from the skin of endangered species

Dressed to kill while knocking all competitors to their knees

If you dare cross them,

You can kiss your ass goodbye

They ruled with violence and an ironclad fist,

Quick to grant anyone a death wish

The relationship between the two became tighter than Krazy Glue

He was now a full-fledged member

Of the cartel crew

Witnessing multi-billion dollar deals being made

And multi-billion dollar debts being paid

Every now and then he was given a cut

And always, he'd say, "You're giving me this for doing what?"

But big man would say, "For simply being my friend."

How could a man be so stupid to chart a course to his own end?

Together they frequented country clubs and exclusive resorts

Little did anyone know he was making secret reports

He was making incredibly detailed reports of his findings

He even had video and audio recordings

He was slowly building a rock-solid case

Never realizing his life was such a precious thing to waste

Now, remember when I told you of the fat lady's song

Okay now here's where his plan suddenly went wrong

It's normal for a drug lord to have his fears

And this drug lord had been in the game for over twenty-five years

His favorite motto was "live by the gun"

And "fully trust no one"

So what do you readers expect?

From gate the drug lord did his own background check

As far as backgrounds go, he didn't have one

And this all lead to forms of accusations and assumptions

From day one he was being watched with care

Audio and video taped followed almost everywhere

Understand that from day one they knew that he was an informer

So keep reading, this shit is hot, but it's gonna get warmer

See what the drug lord did was flip his own script

And into the game he added his special kind of bullshit

They fed him a pipeline of useless information

A placebo, like a pill, that is void of any useful medication

They led the FBI on a wild goose chase

They failed to realize they would never build a case

This situation, no one in the world could prevent

He had been "rolled over by his own government"

To them he was another ordinary black man

To put it bluntly, he was the sacrificial lamb

See, he was just a small fish in a big dish

Only big business can stop big business!

One needs to understand that drugs are here to stay

And the little guy best not get in the big guy's way

Because you better believe if you do

What I'm about to tell you next,

Could easily happen to you

Okay, things went on just as expected

He thought no one in the cartel ever suspected

He figured with this case he could no way lose

Then one day, he was invited to go on a cruise

A party on the boss's 300-foot yacht

He knew he'd rather go but deep inside he knew he better not

On the ship, he noticed it was only him

That's when he realized he was about to become a victim

The boss appeared and said, "I really loved you, kid

But now it's time for you to swim with the squid"

He said, "You have to admit I treated you real nice

But now, I'm gonna have to beat you within an inch of your life!"

He said, "Hold on a minute, let me explain please!"

Then the boss shot him twice in both of his knees

He yelled out loud, "I was only doing my job!"

Then the boss said, "I know. That's what makes this so hard

You betrayed my love and my every trust,

And took my emotions and used them for your own lusts

For that there can be no form of an excuse!

And for a nigga like you, I have no use

So now would you like to make any last remarks?

If not, it's time for me to feed your ass to the sharks

You can make your last pleas to your guardian Lord

Because I'm about to throw your stupid ass overboard!"

For a minute, he thought it was all a bad dream

And the last thing he remembered was letting out a bubble scream

Now remember what I told you straight from the beginning

That to this story, there would be a tragic end

Understand he was never heard from again

And understand he was so naïve to think the FBI could ever be his friend

You may or may not have heard of a story like this before

Oh, and seven weeks later, his body washed ashore

To protect themselves he was labeled a crooked cop

This just doesn't make any kind of sense

Because he was a loyal FBI agent

As to be expected, his country turned its backs on him

And slandered his name to his wife and children

This is an issue of much needed debate

Headlines in the papers read "FBI to Investigate."

It's important, so I think you should know

A person has to work, to eat, to pay the rent

But before you join the police, please read the fine print

Because when you do, you will no doubt discover

The system has no love for black police who go undercover.

A Bad Dream

Like Jonah recalled being in the belly of the whale,

This particular dream I had, I remember in full detail

All that happened to me in this dream I could feel

This dream was only eyes closed from being real

When I woke I was physically drained

Because of this dream I was physically in pain

I'm going to recount this dream with the quickest way to the end

Let me see, what would be the easiest way to begin?

I had just left this private club,

From listening to my favorite jazz band

Before I could get to my car

I was hit from behind and tossed into a van

When awoke, I was tied to a wooden chair

And for some strange reason I had long hair

I attempted to open my eyes and had no luck

I felt like my eyes had been sewn shut

Then in the darkness I heard a raspy voice

It said, "I'm gonna give you a choice

You can tell me the truth, or you can tell me a lie

But I'll be the one to laugh about this and you'll be the one to die."

Then what he did next was done

Just in case I tried to play dumb

He had someone grab my hand and cut off my left thumb

"Now," he said, "I'm gonna ask you six questions

Answer with honesty now," was the voice's suggestion

To question number one, I answered, "I don't know."

My kneecap was crushed with a swift and silent blow

To question number two, my answer was, "I don't care."

My chair became suspended off the ground, by a rope tied to my hair

I answered question three by saying, "There's only one."

Into my mouth, went a hand

Pushing something sharp into my tongue

To answer question number four, I answered, "Sir yes."

Then a long incision was made in the middle of my chest

To question number five, I said, "Okay!"

I felt something poured on my skin and my flesh burned away

To question number six, I simply said, "So?"

Then I felt a hacksaw cutting right through my big toe

My scream was a gurgle from all the blood and sweat

The voice then said, "Your agony's not over yet!

For what you did you're gonna pay

And before the night's over you'll see things my way."

All of a sudden, I heard not another sound

The chair was lowered back down into the ground

I said out loud, "What did I do to deserve this?"

Then the voice said, "You should never have crossed my little sis."

I asked, "Is this is what all this drama is all about?"

"Yes!" he responded, and punched me dead in my mouth

The whole situation was so insane—

Me trying to place this pain with a name

Then a hand reached into my pants and pulled out my dick

The voice then said, "You'd better say a prayer real quick"

At the top of my lungs I begged it to stop

Then I heard a nasty cutting sound and felt wetness around my crotch

He mumbled to himself, "Yeah, my sis will like this"

A gift in this very bottle, that's right, your penis."

I wanted to yell but I couldn't find my vocal cords

Then what came to my mind was a kind of King of Kings and Lord of Lords

With all of my strength I said, "Man, whatever I did I apologize!"

Then I felt something sharp and hot poke through the lids of both my eyes

The pain was driving me out of my mind—

To make matters worse

"I have no dick and I'm fuckin' blind!"

Whoever this woman was I now curse the day that I kissed her

With a burst of anger, I said, "Who the fuck is your sister?"

He laughed and said, "You're such a tough fool"

Then I heard this loud noise sounding like a power tool

With rage he said, "So now you want to be a man?"

That's when I felt the saw cut through my left and right hand

With tears in his voice, he said, "My sister was so young and sweet."

Then I felt the power saw cut off both of my feet

He said, "You mess with me, if you fuck with my family—

And if you fuck with my family, you get me for an enemy."

My sight wasn't totally gone because I saw red—

My spirit left my body as he yelled and blew off my head

The next thing I heard was an ear-splitting scream

As I woke my own self from this horrible bad dream.

Wrong Turn

Once upon a time there was a black lady

That gave birth to a beautiful black baby

At first, he was everything she ever wanted in the whole world

Until years later her desire grew to also have a little girl

In the beginning the man-child was a blessed thing

Staying tied to his mother's side

By an imaginary string

But as he got older his curiosity grew

There came a time where dear old mom didn't know exactly what to do

It was sad she couldn't say, "You'd better straighten up before I tell your dad!"

Because that was something in the house he never had

You see, his father left before the start of the show

And ran like a bitch

Escaping responsibilities, many years ago

Now what's a single mom to do?

Holding down two jobs just to make ends meet

That, in itself is an incredible feat

Since she couldn't be in two places at the same time

Her son was alone, left to the devices of his own mind

Left all alone to consider life's possibilities

Getting his guidance through what he sees on TV

In his environment there is positivity to follow

Most of his role models' philosophies come from *Hustler* or the inside of a liquor bottle

Let me make this fact understood

The Big Brother program didn't come to this part of the hood

So, with testosterone levels high

And mom's fragmented lessons not well learned

This kid's life took a wrong turn

Now, it seems the kid's gone mad with the choice to live his life too fast

Choosing to hang on corners

With shoes, untied, pants hanging off his ass

The normal ways of society, he can't seem to cope

Choosing to earn his income from buying and re-selling dope

Claiming to settle problems with his hands,

But will not hesitate to *bust his gun*

He's been to YDC twice already

And about to go for a third time

Something must be wrong with him for he thinks his life is fine

Deep down, he's unhappy with the life he chose

To escape the pains of his reality

He resorts to snorting powder up his nose

Now, for the real trouble

His twenty-first birthday song has been sung

He thought it was hard being a kid

But the trials of manhood have only just begun

Especially since the sentence he's serving is a 5 to 9

He ended up in a very strange world

One where men like boys and boys act like girls

Years ago he lost all his fear

Not that he was looking for it, but he found it there

From his actions he passed the point of simple repentance

His debt to society had to be paid with a prison sentence

Right here and now you feel it's all going to end

So in need of a friend he grabbed hold of religion

Through his belief, he learned what it is to be a man

So he chose to take advantage of the state educational program

Now there is a light at the end of the tunnel and countless possibilities

All due to the fact that he received his GED

He is now taking college courses

And researching job sources

Preparing himself for the return of his soul

The day the state penal system grants him parole

Through his pent-up years, he had a chance to sort through all the drama

He was even able to build a loving relationship with his dear mama

And till this day, he still doesn't know why he even bothered

But now on a regular basis he's having conversations with his father

So finally, the day of his new beginning has come

He's a black man about to receive his freedom

He once was blind but now he sees

That he alone controls his destiny

As sure as what comes up must come down

A black man can turn his own life around

There is no doubt that if you have played with fire, you have been burned

But remember, one's life is not over, because you took a wrong turn.

Spousal Abuse

This story makes me want to fly loose

One woman's horrid story of spousal abuse

A woman who was soft, quiet, and meek

Oh, you may want to stop reading here, if your stomach is weak

To protect the innocent, names have been changed

But no matter what woman it is, a broken jaw is still the same

So, sit back and breathe, as your anger may increase

While I tell you of a woman, attacked several times, by the same beast

The relationship started on the basis of love

But soon ended up like twelve rounds without the boxing gloves

The first contact came with an open hand slap

Then came the promise that he would never again do that

But what followed next, you probably wouldn't believe

A punch, a kick, an elbow, and a knee

Anyway, time elapsed in between these frontal assaults

So this somehow made her feel like it was her fault

In her mind this abuse was of her own accord

She never thought to go down to the police and file a record

Now Nicky was slim, built, and weighed about one hundred and five pounds

Long hair, pretty face and a voice that made soothing sounds

Basically, the type that a man would want to hold all night long

And in no way, want to beat up on

Nicky should have invested in a live-in nurse

Because the situation didn't get better, in fact it got much worse

Nicky was frightened all the time and unable to think

And to make matters worse, this spouse of hers started to drink

I should stop here but what would be the use?

It's sad, but true, this thing called spousal abuse

Nicky lived her life in sheer terror

To the point where she didn't even want to look in the mirror

Wearing sunglasses to hide her swollen black eyes

She slept with a pillow over her head to muffle her cries

Before I forget, there was a child involved in all of this

For him to separate from the violence was her only wish

She could only imagine the terror he felt inside

Because when the beatings would occur, he would run and hide

Anyway, she always stayed fresh, dipped, ready for his appraisal

Medicine cabinet, full of Band-Aid's, alcohol, and witch hazel

Life with this man was like the "Thrilla in Manilla"

Close at hand, she kept two kinds of pain killers

She couldn't believe the violence in this love that God created

It was like something that constantly escalated

It was like she became afraid of the night

Because in the dark is when hubby usually came home and wanted to fight

In between the abuse, she would count the days

There were several ambulance rides and a few hospital stays

Yes her life was worse than a bad dream

Suffering with injuries like broken ribs and a busted spleen

Nicky's life was engulfed with horror and grief

Twenty-five years old and already missing two or three teeth

But still she wanted to keep all this a hush

Even down to the night her pelvis got crushed

Nicky didn't want to see tomorrow

She had nowhere else to go

She wanted so bad to call a truce

And put an end to this spousal abuse

She thought about suicide because she wanted the abuse to end

She had no one to talk to; she stopped communicating with her friends

When her family saw her bruises, they had a natural born fit

But she told her father, mother, and brothers not to get involved with it

Even putting warrants out for his arrest would fail

Because she would be the one to post bail and bond him out of jail

When in court he would act like Mr. Rogers

With she right by his side, telling the judge she wished to drop the charges

She actually believed getting a divorce would be a sin

She actually believed that she loved and couldn't live without him

So, on she went with her sick life,

A sick husband and even sicker wife

Who had to constantly lie about how she acquired injuries

What kind of life was she living?

Doing nothing but building bad memories

I wonder if her husband knew what his vows were

Oh yeah, that if she attempted to leave, he would grab his gun and kill her

What's a young girl like Nicky to do?

Tell me, if you were she what would you do?

She was in need of some serious help

Like I said before, Nicky was in this thing all be herself

With no way to keep people from knowing

Because the effects of the abuse were clearly showing

When concerned people interjected with their advice

She'd get defensive and say,

"Mind your business. It's my life."

So, the nights included her screams and her wails

Her days continued, with crying and biting fingernails

When he was away from home,

She'd read her child books of Dr. Seuss

But this was no child's play this spousal abuse

Nicky felt as if she were going to go out of her mind

Finally she picked up the phone and called the Battered Women's' Hotline

This started the "help process"

But the secrecy only added to her stress

Daily, she talked to her personal counselor

Who told her she used to be exactly where she were

She said, "First, Nicky, place the blame where blame needs to be

Stand up! Be a woman, no more living on your knees."

She said, "Nicky, no matter where you go or what you do,

No man has the right to ever put his hands on and beat you

Now the first thing we're gonna do,

Is relocate you from your spouse

What does this mean? Pack your bags

'Cause you and your son are moving out of this house

Oh, and don't leave a goodbye note on the door

But leave instead a copy of the restraining order."

She said, "There's one thing you must promise me,

Don't go back once you assume this new identity."

She said, "I have no doubt in your mind you still love him, however,

You're a beautiful human being who deserves to have better."

She said, "Now's your time to do all you can to forget.

To help, flush your wedding ring down the toilet.

If you are a pain freak, go back to him, if that's the case

But it's your life and it's nothing to waste."

Needless to say, this should be no surprise

Now that Mr. Beat Her Up is gone, Nicky's life is on the rise

Nothing can be done is a ruse,

Because a woman can come up from under that thing called spousal abuse.

Me

My spirit has been battered, beaten, and badly bruised

I show my emotions in the form of thirty five tattoos

In the game called survival I knew the don'ts and do's

I didn't choose to live my life miserable and confused

I don't know, maybe I was destined to lose—

But there's no more time for boo-hoo's

The story of my life,

I hear sung in a B.B. King Blues song

So tired of trying to figure out where I went wrong

Because the past is no doubt, long gone

And so shall I be before long

My faith is so strong, so I know all of this is a part of God's plan

I wanted so badly to be a man—

But back then I knew little of WAM

Now I realize I was his greatest fan

Is there really such a thing as freedom in God's kingdom?

Do you see where I'm coming from?

Or am I the one who's dumb?

All I ever knew how to do was run—

But I was an only son and a severe problem

At times life is so intricate—I did as I saw fit

Me, take another hit? Fuck the bullshit!

From now on I'm legit!

It seems as if everyone is against me—including me

Failure's still a possibility with a foundation built on personal tragedy

Who's gonna be the final casualty—me or one of my prodigies?

I do love my babies—but somewhere I went crazy

I let one too many people play me—

And one too many still lives inside me

Now, I finally see it's too late to change fate,

Destined to be great, I saw it in a dream written on God's slate

Still, I struggle with inner debate,

Wanting to lose some of this hate and walk a line that's straight

God, if you're listening, I'm praying this loud

All I want to do is make my mother and father proud

I am a Homosapien of the male gender

But over the years, I conducted myself like a beginner or better said, a *pretender*

Somewhere my life got out of sequence

So, I guess I have to suffer the consequence

I don't want to do drugs or drink anymore

I want to spread love and hope—but I am sure

For every action there is a reaction

I should have utilized my common sense in the greatest fashion

Inside, I cried to be intellectually stimulated

But all I did was keep my spirit medicated

I attempted to mix positives and negatives like oil and water

Running around like a mad man, in need of discipline and order

After the cream rises to the top, what comes next?

Underrated jobs and overrated sex

Perhaps, I need a restriction vest and some powerful sedatives

Because now my mind is full of distorted perspectives

I didn't grow up with dysfunction and was shielded from corruption

God knows, I recognize my blessings each and every one

From having drug-free parents to the births of my four beautiful sons

There's no way I can undo what has already been done

How was I to know my folly would cause me to fail?

In and out of jail

More than likely my soul is condemned to hell

What eats me up inside is knowing the hurt I inflicted along the way

That's why each day I surely ask God's forgiveness when I pray

I hope somehow, they know it wasn't because of them I choose to run

I just thought I was so smart until I realized I was really dumb.

Afterword

Where and how do I begin? At the end of this book and by telling you about me, in brutal, real, and honest truth—I am a drug addicted, convicted felon who borders the line between genius and mad man, which means I am a human being, normal but with major issues.

The title "From the Mind of a Mad WAM" was chosen to introduce me, Waleed Abdul Muhaymin, to you, the reader. I chose *mad* to express my experience in two ways; one, being upset with myself and society and second, my state of mind. I was being driven crazy at times by society's creations which have caused problems for me and those who live in it.

I am going to continue to be real in my writing so that someone who may be travelling my path can learn, not feel alone, and be inspired. For those who have not shared my experience, I hope to open eyes, minds, and hearts to understand and not judge. If I achieve this I will have fulfilled my purpose to transform and elevate.

Peace!

—W.A.M. (2005)

www.ingramcontent.com/pod-product-compliance
Lightning Source LLC
Chambersburg PA
CBHW070457100426
42743CB00010B/1652